I0827705

Ahayah Yasharahla

Simeon, Ephraim and Manasseh

with Dan

By Tara La Sean

The Lord's Prayer

Our Father (Ahayah) which art in Heaven, Hallowed be thy name. Thy kingdom come, Thy will be done in earth, as it is in Heaven. Give us this day our daily bread. And forgive us our debts as we forgive our debtors. And lead us not into temptation, but deliver us from evil: For thine is the kingdom, and the power, and the glory, forever.

Ahayah Bahasham Yashaya Wa Rawach

(In the name of the Father, the Son and the Holy Spirit)

Amen

Shalom Brothers and Sisters!

It gives me great pleasure to present this latest segment of the *My Time With The Most High* workbook series! Much like the first four books of this series which gives Bible students a variety of puzzles, activities and writing prompts to help retain information about topics such as the Creation of the Universe, our history, heritage and the Law, this series is a guide to better understanding the various actions and attributes of the 12 brothers who are the predecessors of all Israelites.

Although this series features many of same types of activities as the original and can be used by learners of all ages, *Ahayah Yasharalah* is geared toward more advanced students. To complete the activities in this section you will need the KJV Bible, The Apocrypha, the Testament of the Twelve Patriarchs and the Book of Jasher (as translated by R.H. Charles).* This section assumes that you have read these records and are at least familiar with the content. As an extra challenge, some activities will require you to search the internet to help answer questions.

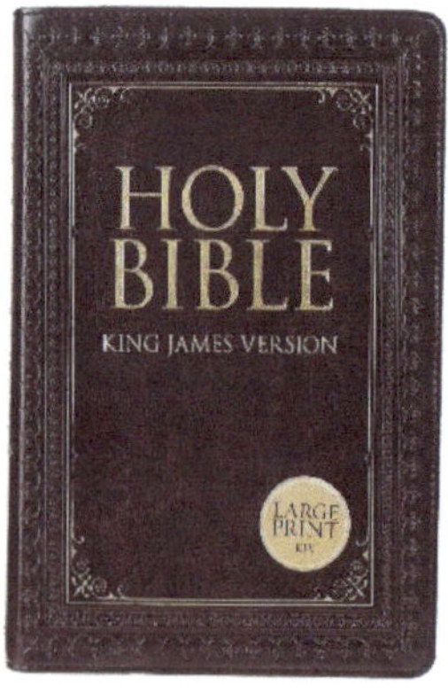

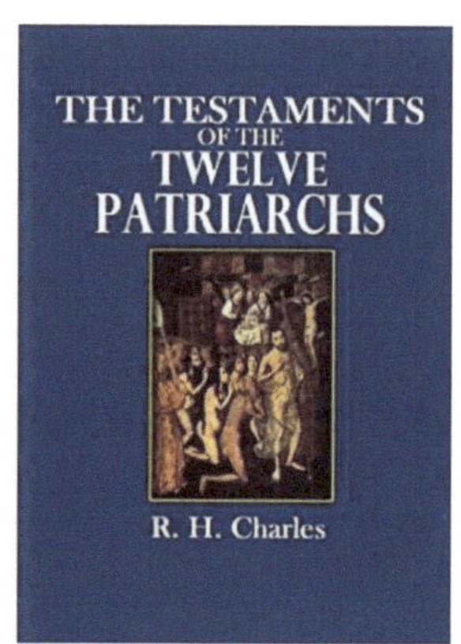

I hope you will continue to study the Word and learn more about our Magnificent Power, Ahayah, as well as our rich history and colorful foreparents!

Barak Atha!

Sis Tara~

*If you do not have these records by R.H. Charles, you can download them for free as a PDF to your personal device.

** The Apocrypha can also be found in the 1611 KJV Bible and the Testament of the Twelve Patriarchs can be found in the Pseudepigrapha.

http://www.earlychristianwritings.com/text/patriarchs-charles.html

http://www.parsontom.com/books/Book%20of%20Jasher.pdf

SIMEON THE BRAVE

Simeon Says...

Complete the crossword using your Hebrew resources.

Created with TheTeachersCorner.net Crossword Puzzle Generator

Across

2. Where did Simeon feel pain after Joseph was sold?
4. Who was Simeon's mother?
6. What two spirits does Simeon warn his children about?
7. What did Joseph accuse Simeon of being?
8. According to Simeon, the ____________ of Israel will glorify Shem. 2 words)
9. Separating from TMH will bring you closer to who?

Down

1. WHat is the mother of all evils according to Simeon?
2. Who did Simeon tell his children to obey? (3 words)
3. Simeon promised his sons if the turned from envy and stiff-neckness they would be like which flowers? (3 words)
5. During which war were Simeon's remains taken to Hebron?

THE BRAVERY OF SIMEON; ROOTED IN WISDOM OR FOLLY?

The Testament of Simeon 2:3 describes Simeon as being strong, brave and fearful of no one. In some cases that bravery was a blessing and helpful to the causes of Israel. But at other times it proved very harmful for the sons of Simeon. Examine Judges chapters 1-3 and Numbers chapter 25 carefully and discuss the actions of the Simeonites in each case. Explain whether you think their use of strength and bravery was wise or foolish?

Closer than Brothers

In Gen. 49, Father Jacob states that Simeon and Levi are brothers, but what is the full meaning of this assessment? Read Gen. 29:31-35 and Chapters 37-39 in the Book of Jasher to get more understanding of this statement. Using Gen. 49 as the backdrop to frame your answers, give at least three examples of why Jacob's words were true.

Not My Brother…

Review Gen. 49 and read Chapters 5 and 7 of the Testament of Simeon carefully then watch the 16-minute YouTube video on Haiti and the Dominican Republic titled "Divided Island: How Haiti and the DR became two worlds." (https://www.youtube.com/watch?v=4WvKeYuwifc&list=PLJ8cMiYb3G5eYGt47YpJcNhILyYLmV-tW&index=2&t=44s) Disregarding the "historical" reasons the author gives to explain the relationship between the two countries, use your biblical knowledge to discuss the root causes of the strife between Levi and Simeon.

Ephraim: First in Joseph

Understanding Ephraim

Read Gen 49, 2 Kings 17 and Hosea 10 and 11 of the KJV to complete the fill-ins.

1. ___________ is the head of the 10 Tribes.

2. Israel is an empty vine, he bringeth forth fruit unto himself: according to the _________ of his fruit he hath increased the altars; ___________to the goodness of his land they have made goodly images.

3. Ye have plowed ________ and reaped iniquity; ye have eaten the fruit of _______.

4. Because Ephraim would not turn back to TMH, _______ would become their king?

5. Ephraim is a fruitful _____________.

6. Therefore shall a _________ arise among they people, and all thy

   ___________ shall be spoiled.

7. And the ______ shall abide in his cities, and shall consume his branches, and devour them, because of their own _____________.

8. And the king of Assyria found ______ in Hoshea;

9. Ephraim __________ me about with lies, and the house of Israel with deceit:

10. The ________have sorely ________ him, and shot at him, and hated him:

All About Ephraim

Find the hidden words associated with the 10 Tribes under Ephraim!

B	S	P	C	B	Z	J	U	F	N	U	T	T	O	C	P	H	U	Y	B
E	F	N	Q	M	C	K	U	M	F	T	N	E	R	D	R	C	H	D	V
V	B	Q	N	O	Z	J	E	R	O	B	O	A	M	Q	W	Z	X	I	S
E	J	N	C	W	R	V	E	N	J	J	U	P	S	C	J	U	D	S	O
R	T	J	A	W	J	M	A	I	R	Y	S	S	A	G	O	O	E	O	M
L	N	Q	L	Q	O	J	Z	V	F	E	B	V	L	W	K	H	I	B	I
A	L	Z	V	V	D	K	C	D	I	L	H	K	U	O	C	Y	P	E	B
S	B	T	E	R	Z	S	T	R	E	N	G	T	H	N	D	Z	I	Y	R
T	C	D	S	H	H	D	D	S	C	S	I	F	R	W	K	I	T	Y	E
I	U	M	N	Y	U	T	S	W	R	A	Q	G	Q	O	D	J	H	P	T
N	Z	Q	F	E	M	I	A	O	L	K	O	F	S	R	N	F	Z	E	H
G	I	Z	U	U	N	A	T	M	B	V	D	U	G	C	N	T	K	I	R
W	N	Y	K	G	O	I	I	P	O	T	K	L	Z	W	F	K	H	I	E
I	J	G	S	Z	N	G	Z	F	U	L	U	F	T	I	U	R	F	A	N
V	R	H	C	E	H	E	V	I	T	P	A	C	A	Y	P	B	G	C	U
N	Z	V	G	T	G	X	G	V	X	G	T	L	G	U	O	D	W	U	P
C	E	O	Y	B	U	T	N	G	S	W	Q	R	G	N	F	J	P	Q	A
N	R	Q	F	E	O	R	J	G	B	G	E	Z	F	Z	I	G	K	M	Q
P	Y	N	Z	I	B	B	A	R	C	H	E	R	S	Q	J	C	W	F	Z
S	J	E	G	H	Y	P	X	K	G	X	F	X	X	T	Q	T	S	M	U

ASSYRIA
JEROBOAM
IDOLS
ARCHERS
ALMIGHTY
BRETHREN
WOMB

NORTHERN
RENT
FRUITFUL
STRENGTH
REMOVED
PROGENITORS
CALVES

CAPTIVE
DISOBEY
BOUGH
BLESSINGS
CROWN
EVERLASTING

Nephilim Beware; Joshua is Here!

JOSHUA: THE QUADRUPLE THREAT!

Most Bible students are familiar with Joshua because he was the successor of Moses who led the Children of Israel into the Promised Land. And while this was no small feat in itself, this brother did many amazing things by the power of TMH! He was an obedient servant under Moses who proved his faith many times; he was a righteous leader delivering fair judgement over the People and (to the surprise of many) was a valiant warrior who bravely fought against mighty foes! Read the following scriptures pertaining to this Ephraimite son and determine which category it fits into and why?

Obedient Servant   Faithful to Ahayah   Valiant Warrior   Righteous Leader

1. Numbers Chapters 13 and 14

____

____

2. Joshua Chapter 10

____

____

3. Joshua 11:15

____

____

4. Jasher Chapter 88: 34-37

____

____

5. Jasher 88: 38-46

____

____

6. Ex. 17:9

____

____

7. Ex 17:13-14

____

____

8. Numbers 17: 18-20

____

____

9. Joshua Chapter 6

____

____

10. Ex. 24:13

____

____

Pride Goeth Before the Fall...

The Tribe of Ephraim is known for having several great qualities such as being brave warriors. In addition to the stories of Joshua, we learn that many men from this clan were celebrated for their prowess in battle. However, like we have seen with the other tribes thus far, there can be a downside to gifts of TMH if we begin to become prideful and vain. Father Jacob warned Ephraim in Genesis 49 that in spite of his strength, he would fall. Read the Book of Jasher chapter 75 to discuss how Ephraim's pride caused their downfall in this situation and why we should never rely on ourselves and our own strengths.

And They Did Evil in the Sight of TMH...

Read 2 Kings 17 carefully. Look at the following sins committed by Ephraim and the Tribes under their rule. Find at least two other scriptures from any Hebrew record that proves these were evil/ wicked deeds.

1. V12: They served idols:

____

____

____

____

____

2. V17: The used divination and enchantments:

____

____

____

____

____

3. V10: And they set them up images:

____

____

____

____

____

4. V17: And they caused their sons and daughters to pass through the fire:

____

____

____

____

____

Is Ephraim really the Puerto Ricans of Today?

There are some Israelites who believe that only the "black" descendants of Jacob faced the curses of Deuteronomy 28. Watch the 10-minute clip of the history of Puerto Rico titled *"1493: Conquest & Colonization of the TAINOS of (Puerto Rico) BORIKEN"* (https://www.youtube.com/watch?v=O3ldlwZF2fs) and give at least **three** detailed examples (with at least **two** scriptures each) which proves they are from the Tribe of Ephraim. Although we can disregard many of the reasons given by the author of this clip for why things happened, the fact that these actions occurred is what we will focus on.

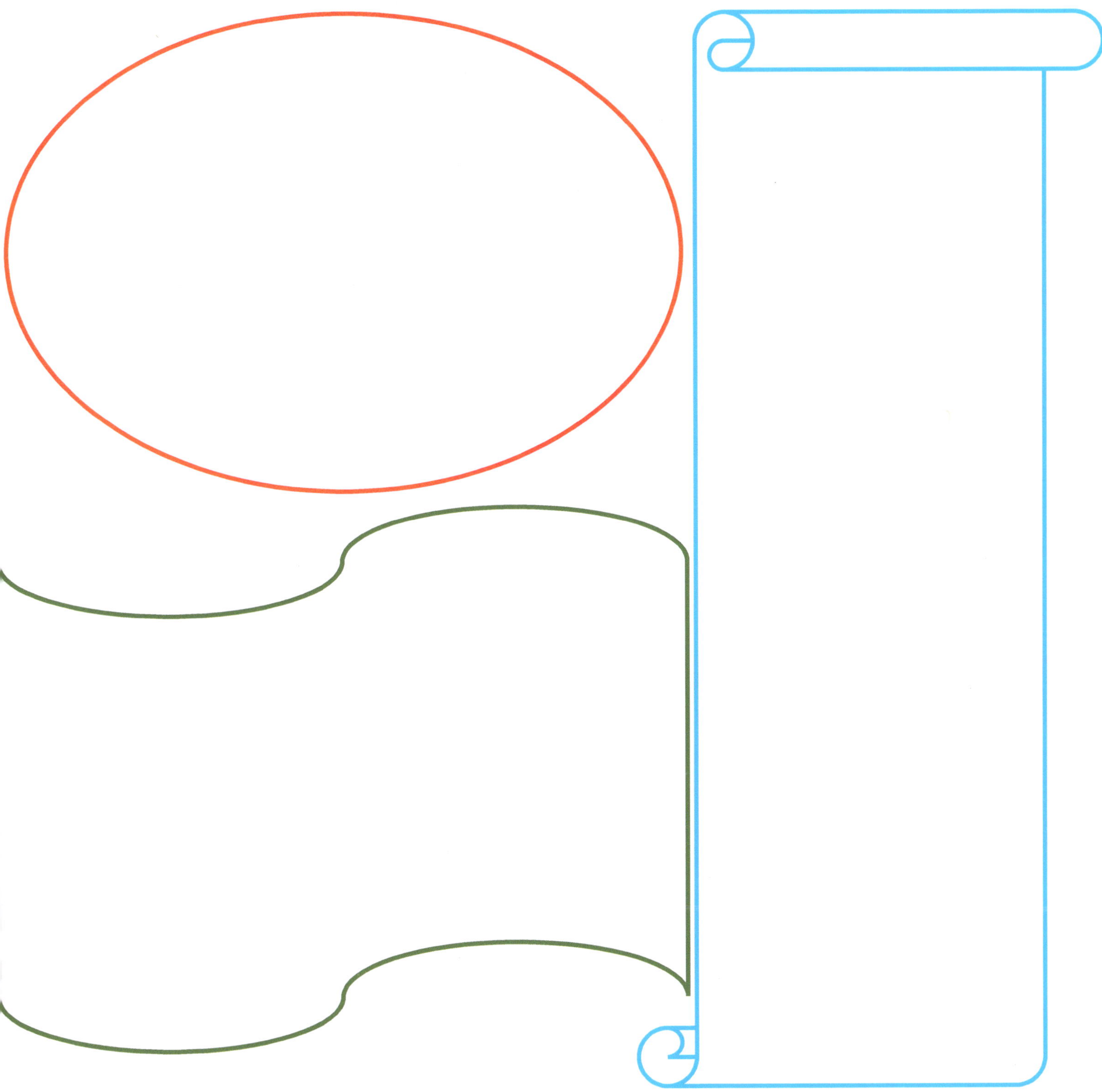

Where Does She Get That Faith?

Like her Ancestral Mother Sarah, Hannah believed that Ahayah would bless her with a child; even in her advanced age. Let's read the remarkable story about this Ephraimite daughter whose great faith was rewarded. See if you can unscramble the words and match them to the correct verse!

She Get it From Her Mama!

Unscramble the word, then write the letter of the correct match next to each problem.

Example:

1. A/ Conceived noccvdeie — a. 1 Samuel Verse 20

2. ________ pihspedrow — b. 1 Samuel 16

3. ________ yadrarevs — c. 1 Samuel 7

4. ________ bertitsens — d. 1 Samuel 18

5. ________ titnoipe — e. 1 Samuel 11

6. ________ vodokerp — f. 1 Samuel 10

7. ________ dwoev — g. 1 Samuel 27

8. ________ candbunae — h. 1 Samuel 6

9. ________ ecantenoucn — i. 1 Samuel 28

Manasseh of Joseph's Fruitful Bough

MANASSEH: JOSEPH'S FIRSTBORN

True/ False

Read the following statements carefully. Use your Hebrew records and what you know about the tribe of Manasseh to determine if the statements are true or false.

_____ 1. Manasseh's mother was Adah.

______ 2. Joseph was happy that Jacob gave Ephraim the blessing of the eldest.

______ 3. Manasseh was born in Egypt.

______ 4. Manasseh's maternal grandfather was a high priest under Levi.

______ 5. Manasseh was part of the 10 Northern Tribes.

______ 6. When Hezekiah invited Israel to join Judah for the Passover, some Manassehites, along with Asher and Zebulun humbled themselves and went to the Feast.

______ 7. The Book of Joshua, chapter 17 details how the Manassehites were able to defeat the Canaanites, Perizites and Rephaites.

______ 8. The prophecies for Ephraim in Genesis 49 do not include the children of Manasseh.

______ 9. His name means that TMH made Joseph forget his toil and his father's house.

______ 10. The four daughters of Zelophehad were allowed to inherit property in Manasseh's portion.

Gideon: Son of Manasseh and Reluctant Hero

Got Gideon?

Read Judges Chapters 6 and 7 to answer the following questions.

Discuss how and why the Midianites began to rule over Israel. Include examples of the ways they oppressed the Israelites.

When Ahayah tells Gideon he is going to save the Israelites, Gideon asks for a sign three times. Discuss what those signs were and what the outcomes were.

Ahayah would not allow Gideon to take many men with him into battle. Discuss the reason why this was so and give an example of past Israelite behavior that proves TMH was righteous to require this.

Imagine That...

Imagine you are with Brother Gideon on the night of his battle against the Midianites; not as a warrior, but as a scribe! You are tasked with writing down the story of what happened in detail. Starting with Judges Chapter 8 as the source of your facts, use your imagination to bring the story to life! Use your best handwriting; future generations are depending on you!

The Real Taino's

The history of the Taino people is a fascinating, although tragic tale. According to world history, the Taino's were part of the Arawak Native tribes living in the Caribbean Sea islands. The term Taino is used to describe all of the indigenous of the region with no distinction between the islands or their inhabitants.

The early history of these people is only archeological overall, and their known existence "begins" with the arrival of the Europeans. What we know about the Taino's (on the surface) is that in 1492 Christopher Columbus arrived, invaded, conquered and destroyed all of the Taino's; The End. At least, that is the story they want us to believe. Let's watch the following YouTube documentary titled **The Last Taino** (https://www.youtube.com/watch?v=I_Qgju9_Opg) to help determine the truth about these native peoples.

But first, let's look at the map below of the Caribbean Islands where the so-called Taino's lived pre-Columbus. Using your Hebrew records as a guide, mark each of the areas with the first initial of the Israelite tribe that lived there.

CUBAN, TAINO OR MANASSEH?

While watching the documentary ***The Last Taino***, look for clues to the real identity of the people who live in Cuba. Observe what they do, how they interact, how they live and the things they say. Also, read the following scriptures to help you determine if these people match the Word. Give examples from the film to support what the passage says. Include additional scriptures to help you prove who they are.

1. Duet. 28:33

   ____
   ____
   ____
   ____

2. Ps. 83:1-6

   ____
   ____
   ____
   ____

3. Duet. 28:62

   ____
   ____
   ____
   ____

4. Gen. 49:22

   ____
   ____
   ____
   ____

5. Duet. 28:30

   ____
   ____
   ____
   ____

What Say You?

After watching the documentary in full and hearing the historians and the Taino Chief speak, do you think the modern-day Cubans/ Taino's know they are the Children of Israel? Discuss why you think they do or don't know and give several examples from the film. While there is no right or wrong answer, include what you think could be done to spread the Word in Cuba given the current social/ political restrictions faced on the island.

Those Island Boyz

Complete the crossword below using your Hebrew records, previous lessons and secular history sources.

Created with TheTeachersCorner.net Crossword Puzzle Generator

Across

1. What is Manasseh often referred to as being? (2 words)
5. Whose prophecies play a key role in identifying who the 12 Tribes are today? (Answer in Hebrew)
8. Which two brothers share an island in the Caribbean? (3 words)
9. Which island is now home to many Massehites?

Down

1. Name the island shared by two brothers.
2. The Taino's are claimed to be part of which 'Indian' family?
3. What two exports was Cuba known for during the Colonial era? (3 words)
4. Which island did Columbus colonize first?
6. Who is Manasseh's mother?
7. Which tribe did the REAL 'Pirates of the Caribbean' come from?

Before Pam Grier Played Coffy...

There was *JUDITH*!

Favored, Faithful and Fearless: Manasseh's Daughter Judith

The Hebrew records are full of stories about faithful sisters, beautiful women and even a few who were undaunted when faced with serious situations. However, no other story features an Israelite woman who epitomizes all of the above in such a unique way. Read the full Book of Judith in the Apocrypha to draw examples of the following terms as they pertain to our spiritually- inspired heroine! Be sure to include the chapter and verse you are using as your reference.

1. **Devoted:**

   ____
   ____
   ____

2. **Virtuous:**

   ____
   ____
   ____

3. **Cunning:**

   ____
   ____
   ____

4. **Diplomatic:**

   ____
   ____
   ____

5. **Respectful:**

   ____
   ____
   ____

6. **Fearless:**

   ____
   ____
   ____

7. **Beautiful**:

   ____
   ____
   ____

AND THEN THERE'S DAN

Dan: The Good, the Bad and the Ugly

Use the Testament o the 12 Patriarchs, Book o Jasher and the KJV to answer the following questions about Dan and his descendants.

1. And ye shall provoke ________________ to wrath and fight against ________________ but ye shall not prevail. (12 Pat.)

2. According to the Book of Jasher, during the battle of Gaash, Dan and which two brothers descended the wall and pursued the inhabitants?

   ____

3. According to Exodus, the sons of Dan were excellent in a particular skillset. Read chapter 36 and describe what that skill was and how it was used righteously.

   ____

   ____

   ____

   ____

4. Read Gen. 49:16 and give at least TWO examples with scriptures on how Dan fulfilled his prophecy.

   ____

   ____

   ____

   ____

5. In the 12 Patriarchs, Dan states that he read the book of which righteous man and learned that Satan would rule over his children? Include what things they would do in the end times.

   ____

   ____

   ____

   ____

   ____

6. According to Dan himself, what role did he play in Joseph's plight?

   ____

   ____

   ____

   ____

An Adder by the Way...

Father Jacob prophesied that Dan would become like a snake that bites a horse's leg and makes the rider fall off. Read Judges 18 and tell how it matches up with this prophecy and the Testament of Dan (especially chapter four) and what it shows about the character of the Danites.

Read the full story of Samson. Examine his life in detail, from being a Nazarene, his relationship with his parents, his ill-fated relationship with Delilah and finally, his end. Tell if you think he was righteous or rebellious in each area of his life.

Wrap- Up

There were so many exciting stories and characters in this edition of Ahayah Yasharalah! Choose ONE person whose story either enlightened you or inspired you. Are they someone you learned to admire, or did they do something you took as a warning? Either way, use the sections below to help you explain why you chose that character.

Who (Is the story about):

____

____

____

What (Did they do/ details):

____

____

____

What Pt. 2 (Can you learn from them)?

____

____

____

When (Did it all happen):

____

____

____

Where (Give location details):

____

____

____

Why (Is it important)?

____

____

____

How (Does it affect you now)?

____

____

____

Shalom Family,

Once again, I pray you all have enjoyed this installment of ***Ahayah Yasharahla*** as much as I did. Our ancestral fathers and mothers were amazing and I learned so many things from each one of them. Although some of their actions were less that noble, I found it encouraging to see how Ahayah continued to love, guide and forgive them time after time.

As with all of the ***My Time With The Most High*** workbooks, activities can be modified to accommodate various learners by working in groups or having the answers given orally instead of in writing. However, this series is targeted at a more mature audience. Where the average grade level for title series is fifth through eighth, these titles are aimed at ninth grade and up.

Before I sign off, I have to give a HUGE thawadah to my church family for all of their love and support throughout these projects. I am extremely grateful for all of the participation from the men and women who helped make this a success! Thawadah to each and every one of you, may The Most High bless you all!

Barak Atham,

Sis. Tara

Answer Keys

Simeon Says...

Complete the crossword below using your Hebrew records.

Across

2. According to Simeon, the ____________ of Israel will glorify Shem. 2 words) (**mighty one**)

3. Separating from TMH will bring you closer to who? (**beliar**)

5. Who was Simeon's mother? (**leah**)

6. What two spirits does Simeon warn his children about? (**deceit and envy**)

8. Simeon promised his sons if the turned from envy and stiff-neckness they would be like which flowers? (3

Down

1. What sin is the mother of all evils according to Simeon? (**fornication**)

4. Who did Simeon tell his children to obey? (3 words) (**levi and judah**)

5. Where did Simeon feel pain after Joseph was sold? (**liver**)

7. What did Joseph accuse Simeon of being? (**spy**)

Understanding Ephraim

Read Gen 49, 2 Kings 17 and Hosea 10 and 11 of the KJV to complete the fill-ins.

Created on TheTeachersCorner.net Fill-in-the-Blank Maker

1. __Ephraim__ is the head of the Ten Tribes.
2. Ye have plowed __wickedness__ and reaped iniquity; ye have eaten the fruit of __lies.__
3. Because Ephraim would not turn back to TMH, __Assyria__ would become their king.
4. Ephraim is a fruitful __bough.__
5. ________ Therefore shall a __tumult__ arise among they people, and all thy __fortresses__ shall be spoiled.
6. And the __sword__ shall abide in his cities, and shall consume his branches , and devour them, because of their own __counsels.__
7. And the king of Assyria found __conspiracy__ in Hosea;

She Get it From Her Mama!

Unscramble the word, then write the letter of the correct match next to each problem.

Created on TheTeachersCorner.net Match-up Maker

1.	a	noccvdeie	a. 1 Samuel Verse 20
2.	i	pihspedrow	b. 1 Samuel 16
3.	h	yadrarevs	c. 1 Samuel 7
4.	f	bertitsens	d. 1 Samuel 18
5.	g	titnoipe	e. 1 Samuel 11
6.	c	vodokerp	f. 1 Samuel 10
7.	e	dwoev	g. 1 Samuel 27
8.	b	candbunae	h. 1 Samuel 6
9.	d	ecantenoucn	i. 1 Samuel 28

Those Island Boyz

Complete the crossword below using your Hebrew records, previous lessons and secular history sources.

						1 h	a	l	f	■	t	r	i	b	e
						i									
	2 a					s									3 s
	r					p		4 h							u
5 y	a	s	h	a	r	a	l	a	h						g
	w					n		i							a
	a					i		t							r
	k					o		i							■
						l				6 a			7 b		a
	8 l	e	v	i	■	a	n	d	■	s	i	m	e	o	n
										e			n		d
										n			j		■
							9 c	u	b	a			a		r
										t			m		u
										h			i		m
													n		

Created with TheTeachersCorner.net Crossword Puzzle Generator